Autumn Leaves

AUTUMN LEAVES.

A LATE VISITOR.

One night of late, when the wild storm was raging,
The city bells had tolled their last night chime,
I, reading by the glow of coal and light of lamp,
Heard, 'mid the voices of that stormy time,
    A low, faint knocking.

I looked not for a "raven lightly tapping,"
But at my door there stood a living child;
An "Arab Knight" looked straight into my eyes,
But muttered only through the tempest wild,
    "I am so hungry."

And when he left with brightened eyes, and hope
Glowing anew through his young, half-starved frame,
'Twas then I asked myself what should I learn
From that weird child uttering one faint claim,
    "I am so hungry."

Oh! Saviour, wearing in our Father's house
Eternal glory on a human brow,
Let me unto Thee come, like that poor child,
For Thou wilt hear the knocking faint and low,
    And "I am hungry."

All in the coldness of a wicked world,
All in the darkness of a heart of sin,
I've been all day where crime and death are found,
I know there's plenty Thy full house within,
    "I am so hungry."

Thou'lt hear me, for "my father was a Syrian
Ready to perish" at Thy mercy's door;
Thou who didst bless the father, bless the child,
Guide me to him, across life's chequered floor,
    "I am so hungry."

Thou hast blest Wisdom for the skilless hand,
Thou hast strong arms for the unsheltered form,
And purity to give for stains of sin,
And love, warm love, for the unpitying storm,
    "I am so hungry."

Oh, Heavenly Father, I must often come,
And take Thy blessing and go forth again,

A pilgrim on the weary march of life,
Pleading amid the winter storm and rain
    That I am hungry.

Oh, let no fear, no barriers intervene,
Between my starving soul and Thy full board;
But more than all, prepare me for the feast,
The marriage supper of Thy Son, my Lord,
    Where none are hungry.

A SONG OF THE FLOWERS.

" Why are you weeping, ye gentle flowers?
  Are ye not blest in your sunny bowers?
  Have you startling dreams that make ye weep,
  When waking up from your holy sleep?"

" Ah! knowest thou not, we fold at night,
  The tears earth drops from her eyelids bright,
  Like a loving mother her griefs are born,
  Lest her tender nurslings should die ere morn,
  And the sweet dew falls in each open cup,
  Till the eyelids of morn are lifted up;
  We unfold our leaves to the sun's bright face,
  And close them up at the night's embrace.

Dost thou ask if grief comes creeping across
From the poplar bough to the dark green moss?
No, round us the sunbeams smile and glow,
Round us the streamlets dance and flow,
And the zephyr comes with its gentle breeze,
To sigh out its life in the young green trees,
And then from the beds where the flowers grow,
Rises a melody soft and low.

And the glorious rose with her flushing face,
And the fuschia with her form of grace,
The balsam bright, and the lupin's crest,
That weaves a roof for the fire fly's nest;
The myrtle clusters, the dahlia tall,
The jessamine fairest among them all;
And the tremulous lips of the lilly's bell,
Join in the music we love so well."

" But startle ye not when the tempests blow?
    Have you no dread of a wily foe?
    Do you not tremble, when serpents hiss
    Mid leaves which the zephyr alone should kiss?"

" Lady, the bells of the fainting flowers,
    Close at the coming of thunder showers;

The branches and tendrils merrily dance,
At the wirldwind's cry, and the lightning's glance.
We dread not to see the snake's back of gold,
Dart through the lilacs or marigold;
For fears that dwell in the human breast,
Find in the heart of flowers no rest.

We have no fears when we hear thee pass,
Over the fold of the tangled grass;
We have no dread when we hear thee breathe,
Over the flowers we love to wreathe,
Nor tremble when night falls from heaven above,
And nature is stillness and earth is love;
We steal from thy keeping when summer is o'er,
And wait thee where flowers can die no more."

THE MAGDALENE.

"Whoso cometh unto Me hath life."

"He goes to Olivet to watch to night,
　　Alone, and weary and dejected,
Oh! dare I follow up the path He goes,
　　What if I be rejected?

If I should be rejected, I who have brought .
  The Captains of the Eagles kneeling,
I who have felt the haughty Herod's arm
  Around me fondly stealing.

If I should be rejected, I who have danced
  Among these marble halls and fountains,
I who have walked with tretrach and with priest,
  These olive groves and mountains.

I who have gazed on stern and passionate men,
  Nor felt one rushing pulse beat higher,
Feel when I look on HIM, as if I gazed
  On the sun's mid-day fire.

He looks upon me with those searching eyes,
  As if He were my elder brother;
Yet wins me to His gentle sermons sweet,
  As if He were my mother.

He says that he must suffer, who are His foes?
  I've walked mid pestilence unharmed,
And from the beautiful brows of those I love,
  I have the fever charmed.

When that dark bearded Roman officer,
  Like a caged eagle lay in prison,

One word from me at day dawn he went forth,
  Like the free sun just risen.

But this poor Nazarene, it seems I can nought,
  For Him, but weep and hear him telling
Of purity, and peace, and deathless love,
  In His own Father's dwellings.

I've heard debates of Scribe and Pharisee,
  And dared to answer them with scorning;
I've talked with Roman Guardsmen by the hour,
  Of Israel's victor morning.

But this man, if He only whispered 'Mary,'
  I could say nothing but 'Rabboni;'
Oh! dare I follow up the path he goes,
  So lonely, rough, and stony.

He goes to Olivet to watch to-night,
  Alone, and weary, and dejected;
I'll follow Him, and say, 'Jesus have mercy,'
  What if I be rejected.?

DEATH OF ZARBARAN, 1500 A.C.

"He lay dying in a monk's cell, but determined to finish for his son a beautiful picture of Christ; he was too much occupied to notice either the monks or his son, answering their questions with saying, "Nothing but Christ." As he put the last stroke to his picture he died."

In the cell of the monks the artist lay,
Dying at close of the Summer day,
Propped up with pillows, his trembling hand
Of the artist's pencil held command;
He felt life's pulse was now ebbing fast,
And each nervous touch may be his last:
Absorbed in his subject, he scarcely heard
The warning voice or the loving word.

"Turn, brother turn, for the holy prayer,
And the anointing oil are there;
We've watched till daylight groweth dim,
To chaunt for thee the appointed hymn,
And the convent bells are ringing now;
Oh! penitent to the blest rood bow—
Up to the crucifix turn thine eyes,
What can suffice thee 'neath worldly skies?"
  "Nothing but Christ, my brother."

"Brother, oh stay thy uplifted hand,
In the glass of thy life is but little sand;
At once to the Holy Mother kneel,
That she may plead for thy lasting weal—
For purgatorial fires await
The soul unshrived at the well-barred gate:
Take warning, thou mayest not enter in—
What can cleanse thy poor soul from sin?"
  "Nothing but Christ, my brother."

Then the tall dark stripling checked his tears,
And the painter's firstborn spoke his fears.

"Father, the glorious old hills of Spain
Are lit with the sunset glow again,
And sister awaits 'neath the bending vine,
  Praying for thee at the holy shrine;
She's counting her beads 'mid the song of birds,
But the sweetest songs are her loving words.
Father, recline on thy firstborn's breast,
Give me one word ere thou takest rest."
  "Nothing but Christ, my son."

"Father, how can I journey home,
When o'er the mountains I lonely rome;
Oh! shall I never behold thee, sire,
Kneeling again 'neath the lofty spire,

Nor hear thy voice up the valley path.
Speak to thy child, 'mid this tempest wrath,
What shall conduct me to thee once more,
Alone, thou'rt nearing an unknown shore."
    " Nothing but Christ, my child."

One more touch and the painting is done,
And the artist's soul is with God's dear Son.

Oh, my Christian brother, be not alarmed,
  'Twas only a picture, I own,
But God can speak through bower and leaf,
  And be heard in fire or stone ;
We lightly talk of men's precious souls,
  And put up *our* bolts and bars,
But we cannot splash in the fount of light,
  Or play among the stars.

One thing is certain, if you and I
  Ever tread on the golden street,
And enter the city with twelve wide gates,
  And stand round the Master's seat,
It will be no form or creed of ours
  Will take us there ; no other
Name but the dying artist's plea,
  " Nothing but Christ, my brother."

THE BATTLE OF RIDGEWAY.

"And God said, have not I commanded thee, only be
strong and of a good courage.—BIBLE.

So God to His soldiers spake
    Upon Jordan's coast,
The true in heart, the strong in faith,
    An undaunted host.
So God to His soldiers spake
    Along Erie's land,
The true in heart, the strong in faith,
    An undaunted band.

Then came the arming in haste,
    And the farewell borne,
From the loving hearts all suffering there,
    On that bright June morn.
On, on, through the weary march
    With a fearless tread;
They went, though they knew before them lay
    The path of the dead.

When suddenly came the foe,
    The skulking wolf hound;
From thence the path of the Volunteer
    Became holy ground;

Bravely they struck the blow;
　　Out their fires burst,
To tell the Fenian horde our word
　　Is "Union Jack first."

No veteran soldiers there,
　　Nor warriors of merit;
All the glory was left for our
　　Brave boys to inherit.
Never before had they seen
　　Their comrades lying—
Stricken down in their manhood's pride,
　　The dead and the dying.

Never had stood in the storm,
　　When war was raging,
Nor felt the bullets like hail
　　In battle's raging;
Yet calmly and steadily on
　　Poured their deadly fire,—
Oh, brave "Queen's Own," oh, gallant "13th,"
　　Shall your fame expire?

There was help almost at hand,—
　　Artillery crashing,
Regiments of soldiers, armed to the teeth,
　　To combat dashing,

Almost at hand; oh, the thrills
Of hope and despair,
That swayed those heroes, loyal hearts,
In that hour of care.

Whoever erred, we know
That those Christian knights
Went with an army of heaven-sent prayers
To those deadly fights;
Given in our churches' walls
To the Lord of hosts,
Given up our hearts' best sacrifice
To the foe-trod coasts.

And God has taught the world,
In the Ridgeway battle,
That not alone by the ball and sword,
And artillery's rattle,
Can He save; but by the might
Of His own strong power,
That nerved the "Queen's Own" and the gallant "13th'
To the victory hour!

THE CATACOMBS OF ROME.

"Mile after mile of graves, but not one word or sign of the gloominess of death."—PROFESSOR DELANNAY.

Mile after mile of graves,
League after league of tombs,
But not one sign of spectre Death,
Waving his shadowy plumes.
Hope, beautiful and bright,
Spanning the arch above,
Faith, gentle overcoming Faith,
And Love, God's best gift, Love.

For early Christians left
Their darlings to their rest,
As mothers leave their little ones
When the sun is in the West.
No mourning robes of black,
No crape upon the doors,
For the victorious palm-bearers
Who tread the golden floors.

Arrayed in garments white,
No mournful dirges pealing,
Waving green branches in their hands,
Around the tomb they're kneeling.

This was their marching song:
"We're not by Death's arms holden,"
And this their glorious funeral hymn:
"Jerusalem the golden."

Mile after mile of graves,
League after league of tombs,
But not one "Saint Maria" stands
Carved in God's jewelled rooms.
No purgatorial dread,
O'er the Apostle's sons,
The early Church no masses sung
Over her martyr'd ones.

Beautiful girls sleep there,
Waiting the Bridegroom's call;
Each lamp is burning brilliantly,
While the night shadows fall.
And baby martyrs passed,
Straight to the great "I Am,"
While sturdier soldiers carved o'er each,
"Victor, God's little lamb."

Mile after mile of graves,
League after league of tombs,
The cross upon each conqueror's breast
Lights up the catacombs.

"'Tis in this sign we conquered,"
    Sounds on their blood-stained track :
"'Tis in this sign we'll conquer,"
    We gladly answer back.

THE WIFE OF HEBER.

"Blessed among women shall she be; she put her hand to
the nail, her right hand to the workman's hammer"
                                              BIBLE.

Rizpah, among her stricken sons,
    Rahab, within the gate,
The dark-eyed gleaner in the fields.
    Of Bethlehem's magistrate,
Mary, who trod at break of day
    Arithmathea's grove,—
All these, and more of record blest,
    We may admire and love.

But do we dare a pattern take
    From scenes with murder rife ?
Shall gentle women learn a tale
    From Heber's fearless wife ?
Shall delicate fingers strive to use
    The rugged iron nail,
Soft hands the workman's hammer grasp,
    The dark foe to assail ?

Not on the battle-field, we urge
  Our direful career,
Nor through the haunts of darkness tread
  To find the foeman near.
Look well within the heart's veiled tent,
  Lurketh no dark foe there?
Pride sleeps; look on his mail-clad form
  Put back the waving hair,

And ask the monitor within
  How oft that haughty form
Hath eat and drank within thy tent
  Refreshed, concealed and warm?
A sterner duty calls thee now
  That sinful brow to brand,
And on the workman's hammer lay
  The trembling, small right hand.

Jealousy, cruel as the grave,
  Hath asked a drink of thee;
Far from the sight of armed men
  The fugitive would flee.
Let slender fingers fearlessly
  The death-charged iron take,
And Jael-like the sleeper slay,
  Ere he again awake.

Anger and Passion, steal they not
  Within the curtained door?
Known but to the All-seeing Eye,
  Those slumberers on the floor.
To us, O God, send honour, truth,
  To keep stern watch and ward,
And let Thy star-gemmed angel, Love,
  Remain our Inner Guard.

"Bless'd among women," we shall hear
  Our holy Captain say,
When He returns a conqueror,
  With Satan for His prey.
Great Master Builder, teach us how,
  Hammer and nail to use,
So that for us a deathless house
  Hereafter Thou shalt choose.

For palms of victory yet await
  Sage matrons, gentle girls;
And crowns of warriors yet shall rest
  On many clustering curls.
Fingers that clasped the nail of Truth,
  Our Prince will not disown;
Hands that the workman's hammer held
  Shall rest within His own.

A TRIBUTE TO THE LOST.

ON THE INTERMENT OF CAPTAIN PLAYNE, P. C. O. B.

" Gather around our comrade,
　Brother officers, all,
The head of a gallant Company
　Slumbers under the pall.
First of our fearless band
　Here, summoned away ;
Comrades in arms, a brother
　Goeth home to day.
　　　　Lift our brother, our brother,
　　　　　Solemnly take him
　　　　Where none other, none other,
　　　　　Passing, shall wake him.

Not in the blood-stained combat,
　The shock of the battle,
Fell he, amid sabre stroke,
　Artillery's rattle.

Had Russia, India, no graves
  In their bosoms deep,
That Canada opens her arms
  To rock him to sleep?
        Lift our brother, our brother,
          Mournfully take him
        Where none other, none other,
          Passing, shall wake him.

When from the shores of England,
  O'er the ocean wild,
The mother in sorrow asks,
  "How did they bury my child?"
We will send an answer back,
  That her son was led
As warriors of Britain go
  To the quiet dead.
        Lift our brother, our brother,
          Lovingly take him
        Where none other, none other,
          Passing, shall wake him.

A soldier, the heavy tramp,
  Of armed men that come,
The thrill of the requiem march,
  The peal of the muffled drum.

But the sword that knew no mark
  Of dishonour's stains,
Lies still o'er a bloodless heart
  And pulseless veins.
        Lift our brother, our brother,
          Martially take him
        Where none other, none other,
          Passing, shall wake him.

A Briton, though far from home,
  The rush of Severn's tide,
Laves not the foreign shore
  Where the loved has died.
But the flag of his country droops
  As our soldier's pall;
Oh, of the true, the beautiful,
  Alas! is this all?
        Lift our brother, our brother,
          Loyally take him
        Where none other, none other,
          Passing, shall wake him.

A Christian; the words of Life
  Have over him been said,
The hope of a joyful morn
  Gleams round our dead.

A light that no darkness dims
  'Mid the sad gloom shines ;
A branch of the Tree of Life .
  With the cypress twines.

> Lift our brother, our brother,
>   Hopefully take him
> Where the voice of his Saviour,
>   Passing, shall wake him.

SILENT WORSHIP.

ON WITNESSING THE DEAF AND DUMB AT PRAYER.

—

'Tis Sabbath eve, the hour of prayer,
· A waiting congregation bow,
They hear no music in the air,
They wait no calm responses low,
Repressed is every smile and sigh,
No words their burning thoughts convey,
'The bended knee, the anxious eye,
They hear not, speak not, yet they pray.

From the dark chambers of each soul,
Through the bright eyes strong reason looks,
No sound of solemn organ's roll,
No Hallowed words from well worn books,
Solemn, Te Deum, glorious hymn,
Kyrie Eleison, humble prayer,
To them are mystic shadows dim,
But angels listen, God is there.

Oh, ear, that boasts thy magic power,
Oh, tongue, that prides thyself in speech,
Draw near unto this silent prayer,
Learn what these worshippers can teach,
Needs our Great teacher ear or tongue,
That He may understand our prayer,
He who hung speechless stars on high,
And makes the silent flowers His care.

Has He not mystic telegraphs?
Reaching from earth to heaven above,
May not these silent builders find,
In His calm temple, rest and love,
And each mysterions untold sign,
Like Jacob's ladder based on earth,
Shall with unuttered glories shine,
And bring down beings of heavenly birth.

Oh, blessed work of charity,
To pour into these minds of night,
The glory of the perfect day,
The blessings of the Holy Light;
Oh, sweet reward, to stand at last,
With these around, no longer dumb,
And hear amid the Archangel's blast,
The Master's welcome, "Faithful, Come."

TWIN DAUGHTERS.

A MOTHER'S IDYL.

Twenty-two years this very day,
  My Alice and Rose were born;
Twelve years ago one started away,
  The other went yestermorn.

I'm all alone in my room to night,
  Yet it seems but one hour ago,
That I kissed good night to two pretty babes,
  In their slumber warm and low.

Rose, my darling! her father's pride,
  She went with the summer leaves;
But she seems mine still, I can hear her voice,
  In the breezes about the eaves.

One went out from her mother's arms,
  Amid sob and wailing low;
The other with music of bridal glee
  And flowers around her brow.

One has only the cemetry damp,
  And dying mosses above;
The other is queen of a stately home,
  And a manly heart of love.

Very grim was the stalwart form,
  Who came for my precious Rose,
But he opened the gates of the garden blest,
  Where the bud of Paradise grows.

Alice has gone with her lover true,
  The light of his home and hall;
So my dear, dead child with the golden curls,
  Is nearest to me after all.

Some day, Alice our household pride,
  Will fold her delicate hands,
And as day declines she'll look out afar,
  To her fair young sister's lands.

Yes, Alice will wait the coming of Rose,
  At the setting of life's sun,
But Rose, in God's garden, will never miss
  The love her sister has won.

TWICE ASLEEP.

I saw the mother lay her darling down,
Drawing the curtains each bright ray to dim,
And with the gentlest accent sooth each sound,
And hushed the loving lips that sang his hymn.
        "Let him sleep on."

How often when some household pet, has laid
All day his aching head upon our breast,
We've heard some kind physician prophecy,
"He'll be all right after a good night's rest,
        Let him sleep on."

We've seen the over wearied turn aside,
And we have darkened up the window pane,
And given a sister's kiss to seal the sleep,
Which shall refresh him, this our hushed refrain,
        "Let him sleep on."

'Tis thus we coax them into slumber sweet;
But when that bed of earth throws back its fold,
And loved ones go, borne out in strangers arms,
Oh, God, how can we say in those damp holds,
        "Let them sleep on."

With strongest tears and cries we try to wake them,
Call them by every name of love they've known,
Give them our warmest kisses, all in vain,
Until we say, faith piercing mould and stone
    " Let them sleep on."

Yet they are ever going, some covered with the blue
And seamless covering of the dark deep sea,
Pillowed upon the mermaid's heaving breast,
Uncoffined in the sea king's cemetry,
    Let them sleep on.

Some in the lonely vault neath cold damp stone,
And many more enjoy a calm repose,
Neath patchwork coverlets of brown and green,
Chequered with wreaths of lilly, violet, rose;
    Let them sleep on.

Are they not like the babe-recruiting life,
Sleeping in peace upon our mother's breast,
Weary with life's long battle, sick at heart,
They'll be all right after a good night's rest,
    Let them sleep on.

When shall the morning come? Easter has past
Year after year, with anthems full of hope,

Yet clay cold feet, are marching to the grave,
Multitudes lying on the mountain slope;
    Let them sleep on.

It shall dawn yet, at midnight the cry cometh;
Soldiers shall grasp their swords, virgins their lampe,
Our angels shall descend down Jacob's ladder,
Till then 'neath drooping banners in their camps,
    Let them sleep on.

LEGEND OF STRASBURG CATHEDRAL.

Out on the quiet midnight air,
  The thrilling summons swells,
As on the eve of loved St. John,
  Peal out the solemn bells;
A city unawakened lies
  Beneath the mournful sound,
Down street and avenue, and lane,
  A silence reigns profound.

But up from vault and mouldering crypt
  Arise a silent band,
Once the true builders of that pile,
  The guardians of their land,

And silently each takes his place;
  Masters, well robed are there—
Craftsmen, Apprentices and each,
  With gavel, compass, square.

Then the old Masons meet again,
  Where once their work was known,
Where in sweet music petrified,
  Stands each well chiselled stone.
With silent presages of love,
  Each doth his brother cheer:
Time honoured salutations pass
  Among Companions dear.

Then on the weird procession moves,
  Through the dim lighted nave,
Adown the long and columned isles,
  Where mystic banners wave.
Over the gleaming marble floor,
  Past the old Knights that keep
Their watch and ward with cross and sword,
  The shadowy Masons sweep.

But near the spire, one female form
  Floats, white-robed, pale and cold,
Mallet and chisel, damp with age,
  Her slender fingers hold.

Loved daughter of the Master, she
  Aided each heavy task,
Beside her father, morn and eve,
  No respite did she ask.

Bread for the hungry Craftsman, she
  Duly prepared and wrought,
And words of Faith, and Hope, and Love
  She to the workmen brought.
Thirsting, she cooled their parching lips;
  Wearied, she heard their sighs,
Fevered, she fanned their throbbing brows—
  Dying, she closed their eyes.

Ghost-like and pale, the once strong men
  Glide over each known spot,
And from the memories of the past,
  Awaken scenes forgot.
No mortal being hath caught the sound,
  Or grasped the palsied hand,
Of they who thus fraternally
  Sweep round each column grand.

Thrice round the olden building, then
  They take their mystic way;
" Happy to meet," they converse hold,
  Till the first dawn of day.

Then down in each sepulchral bed,
  The Masons take their rest,
Till next St. John's loud midnight bell,
  Stirs through each phantom breast.

This is the legend; but far down
  A solemn lesson lies
For all who would their work should stand
  Before the Master's eyes,
A voice from Heaven strews words of hope,
  Round grave, and vault, and sea,
"From labors freed, their works remain,
  They did it unto me."

A MOURNFUL JOURNEY.

"Moreover, I saw in my dream that her children wept, but Mr.
Great Heart and Mr. Valiant for Truth played on the cymbal and harp
for joy."—PILGRIM'S PROGRESS.

We have been down to the river,
  We all must track:
Of the Company of pilgrims,
  One came not back.
The waters were dark and troubled,
  The storm winds blew,
But safely, 'mid shoal and tempest,
  Our loved passed through.

We have been down to the river,
　And the chilling dash
Of the dark drops cling to us yet,
　With their murky splash;
But the victor knew no trembling—
　Only flashes of light,
From the golden gates reflecting
　On garments white.

Only the earnest glance of faith,
　To see if the cross
Glittered upon the brows she loved,—
　All else was dross.
Only the burning kiss of love,
　That the dying give,—
The life-long idol of our hearts,
　Began to live.

We have been down to the river;
　When we thought all o'er,
The sails were backed, the ship returned
　Almost to shore;
And Skill and Love were in waiting,
　To steady the bark,
But from well-wrought hands it bounded
　'Mid breakers dark.

It only returned to tell us
  Of the city fair,
Of the deathless flowers that circle
  Our lost ones there.
It only returned till whirlwind
  And storm swept past,
So with sail full-spread to enter
  In port at last.

We have been down to the river,—
  May God aid us now,
Orphans we stand where the cold earth
  Hides lip and brow,
There came a flashing of glory
  From the golden sands,
And she passed our gentle mother,
  "Father, into Thy hands."

O'ER WEARIED.

Over tired and weary,
  Hand, and heart, and brain,
Seem to pause in their labour,
  Fresh strength to gain;

There's a land where the weary rest,
  Through hours of conscious bliss,
It matters not if I wake,
  In that land, or this.

I know that the iron chains,
  Will all be loosened there,
No more struggling with billows
  Of woe and care;
No more will the mighty ones,
  O'er the abject ride,
Or the priest and Levite walk,
  On the other side.

I am growing weak, oh, say
  Is not the long march done?
Of this life of tempest and woe,
  Is the battle won?
Oh, Father remove thy child,
  To thy land of bliss,
Let my joyful waking be,
  In that land, not this.

But what am I asking for,
  Have I not heard of one,
The Christ, who suffering said,
  "Thy will be done."

Oh, Saviour in human form,
  Foot sore, dust soiled and worn,
Thou didst not turn Thee back,
  From the spear, the thorn.

And I know that of all the host,
  Upon Thy holy ground,
Only the true who endure,
  Are victors crowned;
Ah, these iron chains of care,
  Glow like molten gold,
And this dreary land becomes,
  A sheltering fold.

Over tired and weary,
  Into Thy loving care,
Take me for this long night,
  Grant me this prayer,
To strengthen me for the fight,
  Give me sweet dreams of bliss,
It matters not now if I waken,
  In that land, or this.

———————

THE HEBREW MOTHER.

"They brought young children to Him."

"Salome, sweet Salome, my beautiful wife,
  They tell me thou hast seen,
And listened to the words of this strange man,
  This hunted Nazarene.

What said He to my boy? Come here my child,
  Oh, thou art wondrous fair,
Were His strange arms around thee closely prest,
  His fingers in this hair."

"Dost thou know Him Elnathan?" "Know Him,—
  Once I saw Him, and those eyes
Have haunted the recesses of my soul since then,
  As twilight haunts the skies.

The utterance of those gentle eyes uplifted,
  Seems to say 'I am He,'
Oh, can it be that He is come at last,
  To set His people free.

I cannot bear it long, Salome, this oppression,
  Those Roman Eagles borne,
When only our Lion banners waved,
  Over us night and morn.

I shall grow restive, though the centurion's heart
  Is closely knit to mine,
Caius is one of many, and he loves
  This son of Man divine.

He asked for this our boy, meant He, that I
  For war my son should train,
'Tis said this Man will leave us for a while,
  And then return again.

I think my wife, he must be going away
  For legions of armed men,
If Jesus needs my boy when He returns,
  I'll have him ready then.

' Of such as these the kingdom,' did he speak
  Of David's Royal line?
Weep not Salome, Rome holds the power,
  Thy firstborn yet is thine.

Ours and yet not ours, rememberest thou
  What John the Baptist said,
The day we met him in the wilderness?
  How with a joyful dread,—

He told us of the One who came to him,
  With meekness on His brow,
And when our brother John forbade, He said,
  Yea, let it be so now.

Don't you remember how a glittering Dove,
　　Fluttered when all was done,
And a strange voice was heard, that said,
　　' My well beloved Son.'

And so our beautiful boy was not afraid,
　　But nestled to His breast,
Yet he shrunk back from Caius the other night,
　　Frightened at plume and crest.

"No, no, my husband, there's a fascination
　　Round Him, untold, unpriced;
Let us to-morrow in his footsteps go,
　　And for ourselves know Christ."

TEN THOUSAND MEN TO THE FRONT.

　To the front, to the front,
Ye dauntless sons of a dauntless race!
　　There are foes invading your lands,
　　There are chains for your free-born hands,
　　There are arms prepared to drag
　　From the midway heavens our flag.
Steadily, fearlessly, turn each face,
　To the front, to the front.

To the front, to the front,
Softly and sternly the whisper came,
 In the hour of midnight dim,
 'Mid the merry festal hymn.
 To the side of the dreamer's bed
 It came with a noiseless tread,
And a host were armed at the morning flame
 For the front, for the front.

 Then sang the unshrinking brave,
 "Oh, lead us on to the fight;
 Shoulder to shoulder, side by side,
 We'll stand or fall for the right.
Keep back, keep back, the invading foe,
Our banners will conquer wherever we go.

 Hinder us not, beloved,
 With kisses, and love, and tears,
We shall remember you all when there,—
 Quiet these tremulous fears.
Shoulder to shoulder, we'll crush the foe,
Our banners will conquer wherever we go.

 Side by side with the men
 Of whom Russia tells a tale,
Ranked with the heroes of India's sod
 Who'd have no such word as fail.
We are prepared to withstand the foe,
Our banners will conquer wherever we go."

Arm, ye flower of the land!
Arm, ye brave and fearless band!
Well may we dismiss our fears,
Guarded by such Volunteers,
Blent with that well-tested host
Far from Britain's wave-washed coast.
Tread the proud invader down,
O'er you floats the cross, the crown.

Canada will ne'er forget
How her earnest call was met;
How, in one night's quiet life,
Armies were prepared for strife.
Loyal Irish, Britain's sons,
Canada's undaunted ones,
Forming three-fold cords to chain,
Wolf-hounds and their skulking train.

Fenced with love and many a prayer,
Given unto Jehovah's care,
Go; and if a needs must be
That you rush to battle's sea,
When this peaceful land resounds,
To the clash of warlike sounds,
Charge! for He will by you stand;
Charge for God and fatherland.

LOVE'S REQUITAL.

"Sympathy is lacking from the guilty, such as we, even where angels minister. It is a holy thing to thirst for love's requital."—TUPPER'S PHILOSOPHY.

Who knows his brother's woe?
Who shall go down to the heart's hidden depths,
And slake the fevered souls with streams of love,
Who quench the fierce volcanic fires that burn,
Hidden from human eyes, but One above
    Their thirst can know.

What mortal but hath known,
The pang of parting with some fondly loved,
Their kiss and clasp and sweet words ever gone;
We telegraph in vain, no answer comes,
We thirst for love's requital from the dead,—
    The fount is stone.

Blessed are they who bear
Through this dark wilderness the flags of Love.
I bless Thee, O my God, that around me
The blessed banner hath been always flung,
Though some who hold the cords are safe with Thee
    Till I come there.

The living, loved and sweet,
Are they not with me, near, and dear, and true ?
Does not sweet Friendship head a trusty band,
Friends who have stood by me in stormy hours,
Hospitable doors opened by generous hands
     For my poor feet?

I bless Thee, that the love
Of innocent children hath been always mine ;
They've been like flowers in the path I trace,
And sweetly solemn is the thought that some
Have looked their last of earth upon my face,
     Then gone above.

Oh ! Saviour, in the hour
When Thy parched lips were murmuring "I thirst,"
It was not only for the fountain's flow
That Thou didst crave ; for oh! didst not Thou bear
All the deep thirst for Love Thy loved can know,
     While sin has power.

Oh ! Father, if the sun
Finds me some morning on the earth alone,
Unloved by any human living being,
Loving no mortal woman, man, or child,
Let me die then, God the All-Seeing,—
     Call my work done.

Send me upon the wave,
And amid shipwreck I will seek for life,
Amid the waste of waters I will find a dove,
Amid malignant airs I'll breathe anew;
But when I cease to be loved and to love,
    Give me my grave.

    Why should these doubts enthral?
For Thou hast loved me ; so I may lean back
On thy immutability, by strong arms nursd;
I'll take my cross, go singing on my way,
Knowing that I shall never die of thirst.
    For love's requital.

WANDERING.

"He goeth after that which is lost ti'l He find it."
Lost on the commons wild,
    Strayed from the shepherd's fold,
My fleece all rent with brier and thorn.
    Hungry, dying and cold,
    No one can help me now;
    No one can hear me cry,
Oh, sheep and lambs on the flowery grass,
    Sleep till the morn is nigh.

A hundred were in the fold,
   A hundred went out to play,
When they heard the gentle shepherd's flute
     Calling at dawn of day,
     Led to the vallies green,
     Sheltered from sin's alarms,
Folded oft when weary and faint,
     In the never wearying arms.

Once for his sheep he fought,
   The lion rent brow and side,
But the drops of the wounded shepherd's blood,
     Were but a healing tide,
     Like the drops that flowing fell
     From the stricken desert rock,
His blood washed out the mire and stains
     From the fleeces of his flock.

I know he has missed me, for
   He calleth us each by name,
But never more will he ask for me,
     At the dewy morning's flame;
     He does not want me now,
     Where the wild red roses twine,
For to wait his early gentle call,
     Has he not ninety and nine.

Ninety and nine, who feed
  In the freshly springing grass;
Ninety and nine who rise with joy
    When they hear his footsteps pass,
    And they are doing his will,
    Without a doubt or a fear,
They are following down the path he leads,
    And I am dying here.

  The night is coming on,
    The weary desolate night—
I thought I was strong to dare the foe,
    And brave the lion's might
    Adown the mountain slope,
    I see his fierce eyes flash,
Now through the cold, dark rolling stream
    I hear a sudden splash.

  These are not the lion's paws
    That around me fondly press;
I should know that voice, those kind strong arms
    That so tenderly caress.
    My Shepherd; come down so low
    To save thy wandering lamb,
Back to thy folds and pastures green,
    Oh, take me, "just as I am."

FEEBLE BUILDERS.

"There be four things that be little upon the earth, yet
be they exceeding wise, the conies are a feeble folk, yet they
build their houses in the rocks."—BIBLE.

———

Feeble folk, to dare a dwelling,
Up among the mighty mounts,
Feeding in the springing herbage,
Drinking of the sparkling founts,
And have we no little army,
That the mightier builder mocks,
Yes, we boast our feeble builders,
Building houses in the rocks.

Not our world famed Ctesiphons,
Architects, a skilful horde,
Not our glorious Solomons,
Mighty builders to the Lord;
By the bedside of the dying,
Where affliction loudly knocks,
We have found our feeble builders,
Building houses in the rocks.

Up the bye lanes, in the alleys,
Crouching from the biting cold,
From the mountains, from the vallies,
From the slave ship's crowded hold,

From the cells of many a prison,
Bound no more by bars and locks,
Souls have risen pure and stainless,
To their dwellings in the rocks.

Gentle girls have trod with meekness,
Up life's rough and rugged path,
Loving women borne with patience,
Trouble's drenching storm of wrath
Kings have cast aside their jewels,
Heroes knelt with bay-crowned locks;
Owning that they were but feeble
Builders in the once cleft rocks.

Ah! the world's slaves boast of riches,
Hug their gold and prize their land,
Keep a hundred workmen busy,
Building houses in the sand;
In their hurry trampling down,
Widows, orphans, beggars, all
That would dare impede the progress.
Of each gilded sandstone hall.

Master Builder,—look upon us,
Give us skill to build to Thee,
Every arch and pillar moulded,
Unto Heaven's true symmetry:

Help us, our strength is weakness,
Shield us mid temptation's shocks,
Aid us, for we are but feeble,
Building houses in the rocks.

When the storm of judgment thunders,
Where the sky is blue and fair,
To the everlasting mountains,
Jesu, Master, take us there ;
Lead us to the verdant pastures,
Where thou feed'st thy ransomed flocks,
Owning that thy feeble builders,
Built their houses in the rocks.

ONLY SO TIRED.

"What is the matter with Minnie?
I do not think she is ill,
But she will not run and play,
She longs to be lone and still ;
Doctor, what ails the darling?—
I think she is growing tall,
She has no disease I am certain,
She's only tired, that's all.

She is not like her angel mother,
 You remember how pale and weak
She was, but Minnie's like me;
 Look at the flush on her cheek,
But her little steps come feebly,
 Through garden, bower and hall,
If I ask her what is the matter,
 She's only tired, that's all.

I think that she needs a change,
 Shall I take her to the sea?—
The winter has been so long,
 'T would refresh both her and me;
Young creatures long for the spring,
 And the apple blossoms fall,
Minnie longs to sleep in the grass,
 She's only tired, that's all."—

" My friend, do you see that wreath,
 Of pure and unsullied snow,
It covered a larger space,
 Only one hour ago;
Peep through the greenhouse door,
 At that rosebud sweet and mild,
Tell me what ails wreath and bud,
 I'll tell you what ails your child."

" Doctor, I know that the sun
  Is drawing the snow-wreath up,
I see there's a gnawing worm
  In the rose's crimson cup ;
But Minnie sings her to sleep
  In my arms till the robins call,
She wakes me with softest kisses,
  She's only tired, that's all."

" Ah ! rock her gently to sleep,
  Swans sometimes sing a song,
Give her warm kisses and plenty,
  You'll miss the soft lips ere long ;
Yes, hug her closely, don't grieve,
  You and I must meet such strife,
If we win our crowns my brother,
  After the battle of life.

The worm is all of the earth,
  That lies in your rosebud's cup,
'T' is the Sun of righteousness, friend
  That's drawing your snow-wreath up,
You'll call her asleep and cold,
  When you see a coffin and pall,
But Minnie 'll be wide awake,
  And never be tired, that's all."

RAHAB.

They were standing beside her, those officers in their
    disguise;
Come at their General's command to spy out the country,
Asaph, the captain of thousands; stern lines in his
    forehead,
Told he had borne the command when men's hearts
    were failing;
And led the forlorn hope, in many a fearful encounter.
Heber was younger, but not a less valorous soldier;
And now from the roof of the dwelling noiselessly
    coming,
They stood by a window that looked toward the river
    of Jordan,
Across the far country, where camped lay the Israelite
    army;
And in a low whisper lest any should hear, spoke
    Rahab:
    "Deal kindly with me,
All this good land of vine and olive trees,
These mountains rising up to meet the moon,
These corn fields waving with their harvest load,

This sod with villages and hamlets strewn,
　　　Shall all become your prey,
　　　In no far distant day,
Your military bands shall pour victorious songs.

　　　I know that I shall hear
The thrilling trumpet and the warrior's shout,
Shall these loved haunts be stained with precious blood,
The roses I have twined must pale and die,
For you will conquer in the name of God,　.
　　　Where'er your banner waves;
　　　Foemen fill foemen's graves,
The lion of the tribe of Judah must prevail."

"But how know we, that thou wilt never let
Parent or friend upon this secret seize,
Perhaps there is one within this city, who
Coming to thee in gentle hours like these,
With armour thrown aside, and words of love
From his dark bearded lips, shall by thee prove
　　　This our oath and business."

　　" Soldiers, would I have dared,
Calmly to meet our own king's myrmidons,
And sheltered you through these dark trying hours ;
Had glittering jewels, precious gold, or words

Of warm and passionate love with me had power,
    Think you this heart is fraught
    With one dark treacherous thought,
Towards the army calmly sleeping there.

    My life shall be for yours,
If I betray to parent, lover, friend,
By word, or look, or any mystic sign,
This our strange meeting and the oath you've sworn,
But tell me warrior, how wilt thou keep thine?
    How will your armies know
    I am a friend, no foe,
Can I be safe amid your conquering tribes?"—

    " Our lives for thine, if any of our men
Harm thee or thine, we'll answer for the host ;
Yes, this land will be ours, and when we come
With thund'ring armies upon Jordan's coast,
Bind this long thread of scarlet to this frame,
'T will be the token of a favoured name,
    The men will know it."

    "Soldiers, my father,
Gray hairs are gathering on his temple now,
He may not risk the wild crowd's trampling feet;
My gentle mother, years are on her brow ;

You have had mothers, soldiers, I entreat
  For her, and for my fair
  Young sisters sleeping there,
And for an only brother's life I dare to ask."

" All shall be thine, for we will deal with thee
Kindly and truly as thou hast with us ;
Fear not, the oaths that once we swear, we keep,
And thou wilt keep this symbol safely, thus,
Now fare thee well, our meeting next may be
Amid the clash of swords, through battle's sea.
  This ark rides safely."
The soldiers fled to the mountains, and Rahab, now
  lonely,
Knelt weeping before the blest God of the Israelite
  army,
And praising His name for the courage which He had
  her granted ;
She earnestly prayed for His mighty help for the future.
Ah ! little she dreamt in that hour, how she would
  become
Princess of Moab, she saw in that red cord no token,
That through a long line one of her glorious descendants,
Should give His red blood for creation's mighty salvation,
Nor could she know that her name for a lasting memorial,
Should be carved on God's pillar, with prophets, apostles,
  and martyrs.

OUR RECTOR'S CHRISTMAS GREETING.

Written, on hearing the Pastoral Letter of the Rev. J. G.
GEDDES to his parishioners.

A voice came o'er the waters,
  A message o'er the seas,
Sweet as the breath of Spring's first flowers,
  Refreshing as the breeze ;
A message not of hurry
  Charging our fearless hosts,
To arm and hasten forth to guard
  Our free Canadian coasts,

A voice came o'er the waters,
  "My people," so it said,
And those words embraced a motley group,
  The life-worn hoary head,

Girls with their waving tresses,
  Children with merry feet
Our noble British garrison,
  The poor upon the street.

Men in the pride of manhood,
  Upon whose infant brow
That hand had signed the mystic cross,
  Whose voice was speaking now.

"My people," and our spirits
  Took in the words of cheer,
Read in those hallowed walls the first
  Bright Sabbath of the year.

"My people, as the holy time
Of Christmas feast and church-bell chime
Draws nearer, more and more I feel
Sweet memory's chains around me steal;
I miss you all, each well known face,
I long to fill th' accustomed place;
I feel, though mercies round me pour,
A stranger on a stranger shore.

"My people, two and thirty years,
We've mingled hopes and joys and tears;
And as those sacred hours came round,
We've trod together holy ground.
We've gone unto the manger bed
By angel choirs gently led,
'Mid festive hours we've sought the gem
Cradled in ancient Bethlehem.

"My people, I shall with you be,
In prayer, in hymn and litany,
And as you kneel around the board
In memory of our Blessed Lord,

And take the hallowed bread and wine,
My spirit shall with yours entwine;
We'll meet though seas between us roll,
In the communion of the soul.

"Remember me to all, but speak
Kind words for me unto the weak;
Go to the couch of grief and pain
And give my message o'er again
And tell the poor within each cot,
That by me they are not forgot,
Tell one and all to pray for me,
A wanderer from you o'er the sea.

"My people, through the coming year,
May God's rich blessing give you cheer,
May His blest presence with you be
A shield, a guard, a canopy,
And like the pillar, lead your way,
Unto the land of endless day,
'Till at our Glorious Leader's feet,
The Shepherd and his flock shall meet."

A voice came o'er the waters,
  What shall we answer back,
That telegraph of sympathy
  Across the sea-gull' track?

That prayers his steps have followed
  By way-side, sea and strand,
That warm hearts wait to greet him,
  Home to his native land !

A REMEMRRANCE.

Under the shade of an apple tree,
  Whose blossoms fell, making summer snow,
A group of girls, light-hearted and free,
  Gathered one sunny day, long ago.

Shimmering sun on the waving leaves,
  Shimmering sun on the tossing curls,
As whiling the summer afternoon,
  They talked of their lovers—like other girls.

One heard the murmur of rustling breeze,
  And caught in its whisper an earnest tone,
One, in the cataract's passionate roll,
  Heard warm love told to her alone.

And one saw a youth with raven hair,
  Proudly treading his country's halls;
One saw the light of blue truthful eyes,
  Beaming on her 'neath their cottage walls.

One heard the rush of the wild blue sea,
 And a mariner's voice borne many a mile,
One saw a martial train sweep by,
 And the dearest sight was their leader's smile.

Under the shade of the apple tree,
 Blossoms will fall, making summer snow;
But they whose hearts beat high with glee,
 Are changed and missing, since long ago.

Oh! could we gather this afternoon,
 Would the soft cheeks be of the rose's red?
Called from the mansion, the cot, the sea,
 Called from the prison house of the dead.

Ice cold lips for the coral glow;
 What a change in a few brief years;
Gray hair stealing mid braid and curl,
 Soft cheeks furrowed by floods of tears.

One grows old in a southern home,
 Mid blushing roses, and cooing doves,
One hears the holy words of truth,
 Down the aisles, from the lips she loves.

And one, hush, softly her lot be named,
 Dark clouds oft shadow a brilliant star,

The wandering thoughts of the maniac fail,
  To hide the God, loving near and far.

And *one* the loveliest of our band,
  Draw a veil over the dismal scene;
We all are mortal, we all have sinned,
  And Christ turned not from the Magdalene.

Well, what is the end? That it matters not,
  If we steadily carry God's lamp of love,
Up hill or down hill, 'twill all be right,
  When we reach the summer of life above.

THE ROMAN CENTURION.

Jesus came down from the Judean mountains,
Crowds followed Him along the dusty way,
Tracking His bless'd feet to Capernaum,
Where the next object of his mission lay ;
    " Jesus my servant."

For me beside the city gates, the sentinel,
All helmed and mailed, stands in the burning sun,
To me the undaunted servants of the Tiber,
Come for fresh orders when the day is done,
    One lies a sufferer.

Here in this olden city of Capernaum,
I hold the guard of many armed men,
Roman and Jew known I am no pretender;
Oh, healer of the dying, here me then,
　　'Speak the word only.'

All night the fever raged, delirium triumphed,
Save once, I saw his eye remembered me,
My hand upon his brow, I asked his wants,
His burning lips murmured but one sad plea,.
　　'Jesus of Nazareth.'

That thou should'st come to me I am not worthy,
My glowing armor fires the Eagles fleet,
But pales before the Lion of Judea,
My marble floors are not pure for thy feet.
　　'Speak the word only."

In the stern hour of battle, when the legions
Marched o'er the children of the Nile's proud might,.
The well-aimed spear of the dark browed Egyptian,
Flew at my heart, my soldier checked its flight,
　　'Speak the word only."

Far in hot Nubin's desert I was resting,.
A lion rushed from out his secret lair;

Two eyes beheld it, and the wild beast's talons
From wrist to shoulder laid his strong arm bare,
  'Speak the word only.'

We camped upon the stormy Appennines,
Far up the snowy heights the storm swept by;
I slept, not knowing that his watch-coat carried
Warmth to my veins, Jesus, he may not die,
  'Speak the word only.'

The Roman turned his eyes beseechingly,
Upon the calm gaze of the Lord of death,
And felt a gentle hand laid on his shoulder,
Hope became certainty, Jesus of Nazareth
  Spoke the word only.

BEAUTIFUL LILLY.

Beautiful Lilly wandered in glee,
  With her noble lover close by her side,
And they looked on the blue of the tossing sea,
  And the boats on the tide.

Beautiful Lilly, raise not your eyes
  To that winning smile and that radiant glance:
Look out to the West—for the tempest sweeps,
  And the lightnings dance!

Beautiful Lilly, in your pure soul
　Sweet visions are rising of years to come;
Of earthly skies, where no storm clouds roll
　O'er a peaceful home.

Beautiful Lilly, down in his heart
　He dreams not of altar or ring of gold:
Gather your mantle up—why do you start?
　Does the wind blow cold?

Beautiful Lilly, you'll never bear
　The name of the man on whose arm you lean;
Beautiful Lilly, you'll never wear
　The orange flower, I ween.

Beautiful Lilly, 'tis better far
　That thy dark eyes shadow to hear his name,
Than to bear to thy grave the branded scar
　Of a maiden's shame.

'Died of consumption,'—a common death
　For the budding flowers of earth to die;
And all that's left is the earth scooped out,
　And then heaped up high.

You sleep on the bank of the marshy pool;
　All we can glean from the prairie wide,

3

Is, 'she who was teaching the village school
    Grew paler and died.'

Sleep in thy far away home, dear girl,—
    For no one knows, so no one can tell,
Of love that lies, like a hidden pearl,
    In the heart's deep well.

'Tis only hidden,—some glorious day
    The angels will gather each scattered gem ;
You'll give them your jewel, out of the clay,
    For their diadem.

A FAREWELL TO T. WHITE, Esq., ON HIS LEAVING HAMILTON.

Over the splashing waters bound,
    God speed thee on thy way;
Shield from the grating hidden rocks,
    And the wild breakers' spray.
Command His hosts by sea and land
    Thy journeying feet to bless;
And for thy goodly enterprise,
    God give thee good success.

Going from our Canadian shores,
    Back to thy native ark,
Like the dove with olive branch of peace,
    Over the waters dark.
Teaching the dwellers there, that wealth
    In our land hath birth,
Opening the long closed doors to show
    The treasures of the earth.

Telling of hidden mines that lie
    Deep in the native soil;
Of hundred acre pastures green,
    Waiting the sons of toil.
Of sturdy forests that must bow,
    Before the woodman's stroke;
Of echoes that have never yet
    To British accents woke.

Of darting fish in limpid streams,
    Of pure and gushing founts,
Of valleys rich in fertile store,
    Of towering rocky mounts.
Of thousand birds that sing unheard,
    In their wild woodland nest;
Of thousand flowers that give their bloom,
    Ungathered and unpressed.

But more than all, thou'lt let each know
  That over land and sea,
That flag above their heads shall wave,
  Unsoil'd, untorn and free.
The flag for which *their* soldiers die,
  For which *their* sailors fight,
The glory of their fathers' land,
  Is *ours* by might and right.

Tell them, an open Bible lies
  Before each honest hand,
And God is owned our Father here,
  As in dear motherland.
The same calm prayer at morning dawn,
  Can guide them as they roam,
The same sweet hymn at eventide,
  Can bless their cottage home.

And for thyself, if lonely hours
  Should meet thee on thy way,
And back to distant Hamilton
  Thy weary thoughts should stray;
Remember many a brother's heart
  Awaits thy coming back,
And the mystic telegraphs of love,
  Are with thee on thy track. .

Over the splashing waters bound,
   God speed thee on thy way;
Shield from the hidden grating rocks,
   And the wild breakers' spray.
Command His hosts, by sea and land,
   Thy journeying feet to bless;
And for thy goodly enterprise,
   God give thee good success.

CORONATION OF GODFREY DE BOUILLON.

The conquering army slowly march,
Beneath the castle's lofty arch,
Thousands of trusty knights passed on,
Whose swords the Holy Land had won;
Some with the yet unhealed scar
Left by the Turkish scimitar,
Each with the sharpened lance at rest—
Each with the cross upon his breast.

They with the music's thrilling strain,
Here crossed the brook, the field, the plain
And chaunted forth their leader's fame—
Godfrey de Bouillon's magic name;

Now with the crown and signet ring,
They come to hail their victor king,
And wreathe with bay and sparkling gem
The monarch of Jerusalem.

Forth stepped their leader, and a shout,
That thrilled his very soul rang out;
Then as on high he raised his hand,
Silence fell o'er the martial band —
A pause in bugle, trump and song,
A stillness o'er thé mighty throng,
A single voice the silence broke—
Godfrey de Bouillon gently spoke.

" Oh, Knights, companions, dauntless hearts.
    That by my side have stood
And won the Holy Sepulchre,
    'Mid seas of fire and blood,
Here hail me as your brother, friend;
    To your encampment bring
Me as your loved, true, trusty friend,
    But crown me not your King.

Friends and companions we have met
    Upon the tented ground,
Honor and love and charity
    Have in your camp been found;

We've drank at Sychar's ancient well,
　We've camped on Zion's hill;
Look, knights, the lion keeps his paw
　Upon the Crescent still.

But oh, dear knights, forget not, we
．Are followers of One
Who for *our* sakes bowed down to death,
　As He the victory won.
Honoured am I, His hosts to lead,
　To Olivet's dark shade—
To suffer where He suffered pain,
　To pray where He has prayed.

Friends and companions, not to me
　Shall be this homage given,
I dare not here be crowned a King
　Where wept the King of Heaven;
Shall steel and iron weld for Him,
　And gold for me entwine;
Shall the Thorn Acacia wreath His brows,
　And the soft laurels mine?

Adown these streets, He wearily
　Mocked by the soldiers, went;
'Mongst yonder trees in midnight hours
　In agony He bent;

Upon that Mount He wept in grief,
  By that dark murmuring spring
Walked the cross-bearing Nazarene,
  Oh, crown me not its King.

Sir Knights within these city gates,
  Solomon's temple rose,
And strength and beauty still kept guard
  Despite their many foes;
The Crescent we must keep in check,
  But crowns may not entwine
Around our brow, till Christ comes back
  To Holy Palestine.

Oh, by the life which He laid down,
  His agony and pain,
May we be ready to go forth
  In His triumphant train;
Back to your altars, Christians, Knights,
  There kneeling humbly pray
Godfrey de Bouillon may be found
  Meet for his crown that day."

BEFORE THE BALL.

—

I must lead this dance to-night;
'Mid rustle of satin and showers of pearls,
And on me will be turned the beaming eyes
    Of those lovely girls.

And my very lightest word
Will be cherished and talked over days to come,
And all but the favoured few will wish
    The few were at home.

They'll robe for this ball to night,
Thinking the while of this jewel and star,
Little dreaming the wearer's heart
    Is away so far.

Perhaps for them, fair vain things
The strife of hearts hath but just begun,
But for him on whose arm they will lean to-night,
    The battle is done.

And life takes another hue
When love's medal is turn'd by time's sweeping tide
And we learn to decipher the mystic words
    On the other side.

Oh! for one pair of eyes
That will not look on me this many a night,
And the dear small hand and the soft red lips,
    All veiled from my sight.

    Back, dreams of the restless past,
Down to the depths of my deep strong heart,
What doth it boot? There are crooked lines
    Upon every chart.

I must lead the dance to-night,
And remember a thousand foolish things,
'Tis kind to flatter and gently soothe
    Life's jarring strings.

I suppose it is a truth
That for every idle word which we speak
We must answer *the e*, where no falsehoods gloss
    The strong or the weak.

Well, I must lead this dance.—
The stone at the sepulchre's door I see,
Some day the angels will roll it away,
    And the slave go free.

LOOKING ONWARD.

We're encamping in the valley,
'Mid the shadows dark and dim;
Captain, in Thy glorious dwelling,
Hear Thy soldier's pleading hymn:
Hasten back! Thy troops await Thee,
Foes are round us, near our camps;
We, while war is raging wildly,
Grasp our swords and trim our lamps.

All adown the olden ages,
Notched upon the rocks of time,
There hath echoed one low murmur,
Soft, subdued, like vesper's chime.
From the ranks of earth's o'er-wearied,
Million voices swell the hum;
And the sad refrain is worded.—
"Captain of Salvation, Come!"

Round our earth-camp flows a river,
Turbid, dark, and swol'n the streams;
On the other side the river
Our comrades' armour gleams.

Now and then we hear a splashing—
Lo! one from our ranks has passed,
When the right wing of the army
Waits the Grand Archangel's blast.

Sometimes baby hands, that firmly
Grasp their tiny, glittering swords,
In the Captain's strength made perfect,
O'er the dark foe and his hords.
With the bright cross on each forehead,
Damp with fresh baptismal dew,
They have heard the joyful whisper—
" Loved ones, I am waiting you."

Sometimes men, who bear their honours
Meekly on each aged breast;
They have trained the young for battle,
Then are called to take their rest.
Rest, and with it high promotion,
Blessed guards about our King,
Daily gathering from our armies,
While we watch the day-star's spring.

We are waiting, in the darkness.
For the dawning of the light;
As the sentries pass we ask them,—
" Watchman, tell us of the night?"

And they give us mystic passwords,
'Fear,' and 'Watchfulness,' and 'Hope;'
We are resting on our armour,
Till light gilds the mountain slope.

Sometimes sounds the noise of chariots,
And the roll of conquerors' drums;
Then along the lines there echo
Whispers loud, "He comes! He comes!'
But the murmurs die in silence,
And the roll faints on the breeze,
While the ensigns droop the banners,
And the soldiers stand at ease.

Ah, not always shall we vainly
Watch for our beloved's return,
Soon upon the mountain summit,
Shall the fires of warning burn,
Courage comrades, wait the battle,
Hark! a loud, a martial hum,
See there's light upon the flagstaff,
"Captain of Salvation," Come!

OUR POOR BRETHREN.

"Our poor and penniless brethren dispersed over land and sea."—MASONIC SENTIMENT.

They met in the festive hall,
　　Lamps in their brightness shone,
And merry music, and mirth,
　　Aided the feast of St. John;
Men pledged the health of their Queen,
　　And of all the Royal band,
The flags of a thousand years,
　　The swords of their mother land.

Then mid the revelry, came
　　The sound of a mournful strain,
Like a minor chord in music,
　　A sweet but sad refrain;
It rose on the heated air,
　　Like a mourner's earnest plea,
" Our poor and penniless brethren,
　　Dispersed over land and sea."

Poor and penniless brethren,
　　Scattered over the world,
Want, and misfortune, and woe,
　　Round them fierce darts have hurled;

Wandering alone upon mountains,
  Sick, and fainting, and cold,
Lying heart-broken in prison,
  Chained in an enemy's hold.

Dying on fields of combat,
  With none to answer back,
The masonic sign of distress,
  Left on the battle's track,
Shipwrecked in foaming waters,
  Clinging to broken spars,
Dying this night of St. John,
  'Mid the ocean and the stars.

Others with hunger faint, we
  Taste these rich and varied meats,
Oppression gives them no home,
  But dark and desolate streets ;
Oh, God of mercy, hear us,
  We ask a boon from Thee,
For poor and penniless brethren,
  Dispersed over land and sea.

Poor and penniless brethren,
  Ah, in the Master's sight,
We all lay claim to the title,
  On this our Festival night;

Lone pilgrims journeying on
  Towards light that streams above,
Treading the chequered earthworks,
  Till we reach the land above.

Work up to the landmark brethren,
  We shall not always stay,
The falling shadows warn us,
  To work in the light of day,
How often our footsteps turn,
  Where a brother's form is hid,
Oft we fling evergreen sprays,
  On a brother's coffin lid.

Thou who did'st give to each,
  Some appointed post to hold,
To cherish the suffering and weak,
  To give Thy silver and gold,
To guard as a soldier guards,
  Honour and Love's pure shrine,
To give our lives for others,
  As Thou for us, gave Thine.

To Masons all over the world,
  Give wisdom to work aright,
That they may gather in peace,
  Their working tools at night;

May Love's star glitter o'er each,
　'Mid the world's surrounding mist,
As it gleams this night of St. John,
　"Holy Evangelist."

A SOLDIER'S STORY.

"You ask of my comrade, lady.
　It is a story often told
Of the heated in the battle,
　Growing suddenly cold.
He was as fine a soldier
　As in any ranks you'd meet—
So wise, so good, so fearless,
　Here is his ' *carte de visite.*'

Yes, his hair fell in just those waves
　See how his red lips smile;
Ah, we bivouacked together;
　We wandered many a mile—
Yes, 't was a rifle's fire
　Laid Harry within the tent;
It was hard to catch his accents,
　As over his form I bent.

I spoke of his home, his loved,
  That were far off—many miles;
I whispered of promotion,
  And his pale lips wreathed with smiles."
"I'm sure of promotion, Charley,
  And you'll be promoted too,
Faithful comrade—be ready—
  Meet me at the Grand Review.

When the Great Commander comes,
  With blood-red banners o'er head,
There'll be men and officers plenty
  Reported, missing and dead.
Don't be faint-hearted, Charley,
  Though the road lies up the hill—
Though you hav'nt yet tried the armor,
  And don't yet know your drill.

I know you'll enlist yet, Charley,
  The sword will flash on your side,
You'll bind the cross on your breast,
  And on to victory ride.
The Captain is waiting, Charley,
  In shade of Golgotha's Hill,
And the Heavenly Adjutant, Charley,
  Will see that you're taught your drill.

Only a little endurance—
  Like that you've shewn in the strife.;
And, Charley, there waits your coming—
  Promotion and endless life;
Only a few more watchings,
  'Mid the darkness and the damp—
Only a few more pacings—
  Round and about the camp.

And well I know, dear comrade,
  When the last *reveille* is blown,
There'll be men and officers plenty,
  To file round the Jaspar Throne
Only,"——'t was all I heard, lady;
  On this arm lay a curly head;
And the officer on guard,
  Reported my Harry dead.

Many long years have vanished
  Since we fired o'er Harry's bier;
And I'm hearing the "sun-set" call
  Which he died too young to hear.
But I've found the Captain, lady,
  Who is loving my Harry still;
And from the Heavenly Adjutant,
  Slowly, I'm learning my drill.

I'm only struggling now, lady,
  With the tempest and the strife,
Till the bugler in black armor
  Blows the "lights-out" call of life.
And when in the morning wakening,
  I hear the last trumpet blown,
I'll fall into rank with Harry,
  And file round the Jaspar Throne."

THE STARLIGHT.

"They carried him gently, Rachel holding his hand in hers.
It was soon a funeral procession; the star had shewn him
where to find the God of the poor.—DICKENS 'HARD TIMES.'

" Will you please gently set me down?
  I've a few words to speak,
To her who holds her hand in mine,
  I feel I'm growing weak ;
Thank'ee my friends, I know what e'er
  Has passed in days gone by,
You never took me for a thief,
  Under God's blessed sky.

Rachel, the time of parting comes,
　　No more nice moonlight walks,
After the Works are all shut up,
　　And no more quiet talks.
Oh, the long years we've loved in vain,
　　I'm going where all is fair,
They hunger not, nor faint with cold,
　　They need no money there.

Rachel my love, 'twas hard when all
　　The old hands turned away,
The men I worked with many a year,
　　And stood by night and day,
I never would combine, my love,
　　I kept the promise fast,
I made you then, the boys will find
　　I was not wrong, at last.

'Tis all a muddle, Rachel dear,
　　I cannot make it out,
The Squire 'll see me righted yet,
　　And God is good, no doubt;
I'm sorry for the Squire, dear,
　　Ah, low his poor heart sank,
When the truth flashed plainly on his mind
　　His *own son* robbed the Bank.

'Tis all a muddle; where is she?
  Does the poor wretch yet live?
Rachel, my angel, in this hour
  I've learnt to say 'forgive.'
I cannot speak again of her,
  Rachel my own, my life,
May *we* not on the other side,
  Meet God as man and wife.

Rachel my child, look at that star,
  I think 'twill lead me home,
It watched me many a weary hour,
  Last night it whispered come;
I think it is the very star
  That showed our Saviour's bed;
Sometimes at nights, look out for it,
  When I am with the dead.

God bless thee for that pure true love,
  That kept my soul from sin,
I'll tell the keeper of the gate
  You're ready to come in;
I'm not afraid to go, Rachel,
  Christ died, I trust His grace,
Where are my friends? let them move on;
  Jem, cover up my face."

Gently, and on with measured step,
   The rough men slowly moved,
A silence, and they halt to rest,
   The man they truly loved ;
With heads uncovered then they stood,
   And each one held his breath,
The star had lit the ' oldest hand '
   Across the waves of death.

CONTENTS.